RELIGION IN PUBLIC INSTRUCTION.

BACCALAUREATE ADDRESS,

DELIVERED BEFORE

THE GRADUATING CLASS

OF

ANTIOCH COLLEGE,

YELLOW SPRINGS, OHIO,

JUNE 20, 1860.

BY

THOMAS HILL.

BOSTON:
LITTLE, BROWN AND COMPANY.
1860.

CAMBRIDGE:
Allen and Farnham, Printers.

ADDRESS.

I HAVE long felt that the greatest need in our systems of education is the need of well-established principles in regard to the selection of a course of studies. Could we determine upon sure grounds, what are the fundamentals of a liberal education, and in what proportion they ought to occupy the student's mind, the theory of instruction would have a firm basis, and we could rapidly advance towards perfection in the practice. In the hope of stimulating more effective laborers to work upon this problem, I have frequently recurred to it upon public occasions, treating of various parts of it according to the demands of the hour.

I propose, to-day, to take up the inquiry, To what extent and in what form should Religion enter into the scheme of public instruction? Shall our public schools be thoroughly secularized, and religious instruction be reserved exclusively for the Sunday school and the pulpit? Or shall our schools become sectarian, and indoctrinate the pupils in the tenets of that sect to which a majority in the school district may chance to belong? The questions of Bible or no Bible, of King James' or the Douay version, now agitating in some parts of our country the public mind, are but parts of this greater question, whether in our schools we are with the "positivist" to ignore God, with the Atheist to deny his existence, with the Pantheist to dream that we ourselves are God, or with the Hebrew, to reverence and adore Him.

Religious questions, being by universal consent the most vital of all, naturally engender most heat in their discussion. In proportion as a subject appeals to deeper and more vital parts of our nature, we feel the more interest in opinions upon it, and cling with more tenacity and earnestness to our own conclusions.

This is evident, not only on a comparison of religious questions with others, but on a comparison of any two branches of the great hierarchy of sciences, or indeed, even upon a comparison of the different classes of study in each branch; as I might readily illustrate by all the great contests upon disputed questions in mathematics, physics, history, politics, or religion. The heat of the battle has always been proportioned to the elevation of the subject in the hierarchy, or to the relation which it bore to metaphysical and religious questions. Those questions which have referred only to space, to what is external to the soul, have never elicited heat in the discussion, even when they have been incapable of solution. The dispute has in such cases sometimes seemed interminable, but it has not aroused any feeling, at least not any to be compared with the intense zeal of the politician, the fierceness of metaphysicians, or the bigoted fury of theologians.

I am therefore aware that in approaching this question, of the place which religion should hold in a course of public instruction, I am approaching dangerous ground. It may be impossible for me to consider it without myself betraying a feeling that may seem inconsistent with impartial judgment, or else exciting feelings in others which will prevent some from seeing my errors if I err, and others from acknowledging the force of my conclusions if I arrive at truths.

Suffer me, therefore, to leave, at first, the path in which I propose finally to approach those conclusions; and to discuss, for a few moments, the question, To what extent and in what form should geometry enter into a course of public instruction? By thus going to the opposite end of the scale of sciences, and discussing the question with reference to the simplest and most elementary science, we may arrive, perchance, coolly at principles which will be found applicable at every point of the scale, and which may guide us safely when we approach the more exciting question of religious instruction.

Shall we admit geometry into the ordinary course of

public instruction, or shall we reject it? Of course we shall admit it. But upon what grounds? I answer, because it is a fundamental branch of the hierarchy, and the knowledge of any thing whatever implies some knowledge of the truths and relations of space. To what extent shall we admit it? I answer, that it should be introduced to a sufficient extent to prepare the student for all the studies in the public course, at all dependent on geometry; but it must not be pursued to an extent sufficient to crowd out or exclude the studies for which it is a preparation. A due harmony and proportion must be maintained in the branches taught, and in deciding what this due proportion is, we must take into account the length and breadth of the curriculum, and the native powers and peculiar circumstances of the individual whose tuition is under consideration.

Then, in what form shall geometry be introduced? — as abstract science or as practical rule? — in theorems or in problems? and if in problems, shall they be solved by construction, or by calculation and analysis? I answer, that the method of nature is to rise from examples to principles, and that geometry should be presented first in concrete form to the eye and to the imagination, and made a matter of construction; afterward the pupil should be lifted up to a scientific and even to a metaphysical view of the abstract relations of space. The proportions in which these modes of presenting geometry should be employed, will vary with the length of the curriculum, or course of studies, and be adapted somewhat to individual circumstances, but the ruling principle will always be the same, namely, to give so much and such geometrical training as will prepare the pupil, as well as his powers and his circumstances will admit, for an understanding of the full circle of sciences, and thus for the fulfilment of all the duties of his station in life.

The answers which I have thus given concerning the science of geometry will be acknowledged, I think, by all educators to be, in the main, sound; and the practice of all schools and colleges in the world is in essential conformity thereto. In some institutions geometry may be neglected, in others over-cultivated; in some treated too abstractly, in others made too much a mere matter of drawing with compass and ruler; but all this arises from errors of judgment in applying the fundamental principles of education to the question, and not from any doubt concerning the principles themselves.

Turning now to the main object of my discourse, I ask, Shall religion be introduced into the course of public instruction, or shall it be utterly excluded? And the answer seems to me plain, that we must admit it. Even in an intellectual point of view, theology is one of the fundamental branches of the hierarchy of sciences, and so completely interwoven with the rest, that we do not and cannot fully comprehend any one of them, until we have traced it in its relations to theology.

Begin with the simplest of all branches, the mathematics, and a moment's reflection will show how utterly worthless they are in every other light than this, that they alone give us a knowledge of the exactness of God's thought, and alone are capable of demonstrating to us, from the manifestation of thought in the creation, the necessity of supposing the existence of a Thinker. In using the mathematics for this purpose, of discovering the harmonies of creation, and for testing the infinite perfection of nature's works, we have the most effective means of improving the mathematics themselves.

Thus, all great improvements in the sciences of space and time have arisen from some effort to solve the problems suggested by the works of nature; and a large proportion of them have been made by those who were stimulated to the solution of these problems by the faith that they thereby came into communion with the thoughts of the Most High.

In like manner, physics are not carried to their true conclusions until they lead us to speculate concerning the origin of matter, and to trace the designs and plans of the Architect of the universe; and, on the other hand, these teleological and morphological speculations have borne their natural fruit, in leading to wider and more exact views of the physical sciences. In illustration of this statement, I would simply refer to two of the greatest of all names in zoölogy, which is the crowning division of physical sciences; to Cuvier, who was led to his wondrous discoveries by his steady adherence to the axiom, that every organ was intelligently adapted to its functions; and to Agassiz, who could advance beyond his master only by taking a still higher religious view, and assuming that every variation in animal forms, and every succession in those variations, is in fulfilment of one comprehensive plan of the Divine thought.

When we ascend into historical studies, their incompleteness, when treated independently of their relations to theology, is still more apparent. How poor would be the narrative of the growth of the arts of life, if we did not recognize the adaptation of the physical world to the needs of man, and the beneficence of the divine Creator in that adaptation. How unsatisfactory our enjoyment of art, and how defective our survey of the field of æsthetics, did we not perceive here also the tokens of a divine nature in man, which makes him capable of appreciating the mind of God, as manifested in the forms and colors and tones of the material world. The music of nature is adapted to man; and our knowledge of music is not complete until we have perceived this adaptation, and seen that it arises from the kindness of a beneficent Creator. Thus, also, is philology incomplete, unless it leads upward to theology. What are the various languages of man but so many barbarous dialects, until the clear light of a religious mind is thrown upon the study of words, and we are taught to hear in the sounds of human speech — so simple in their elements, so infinitely various in their combinations — the proofs of a Divine Providence, and to trace, in the development and growth of languages, the plan of an infinitely wise Teacher, carried out, like his plans concerning the material world, by the means of exceedingly simple but efficient laws? And in the sciences of political economy and law, in the history of governments and of nations, what order or what completeness can there be in the studies of one who does not seek the footsteps of God in history, — who does not recognize the paternal character of God, and the wisdom of his plans for the development of races, as the fundamental axioms of historical research?

Nor, finally, is the study of the human mind complete, unless it leads us to the study of theology, and is guided by the light which is from above. No man can possibly view the human soul aright, who looks upon it either as the highest manifestation of matter, or as the highest possible manifestation of spirit. Then only can we understand ourselves aright, when we find in our own minds feebler glimmerings of that infinite wisdom which guides alike the atoms and the planets, — fainter emotions of that unfathomable love which has filled the universe with its myriads of happy creatures. Then only is the study of the human mind vested with its highest dignity and interest, when we perceive that in studying ourselves, we are studying also Him whom we can never fully comprehend, but who has, both in creation and in the revelation through prophets and apostles, declared that we were made in his image.

Thus self-evident do I hold it to be, that theology is a fundamental branch, the crown and glory of all the hierarchy of sciences, and that no one branch is, or can be, understood in full, until we have traced its relations to theology.

If, therefore, we would have our course of public instruction possess any thing like even intellectual completeness, it must embrace, from the earliest school to the college and university, a proper proportion of religious teaching.

And that proportion is to be found, so far as relates to the simple intellectual question, in the same manner as we find it for geometry. It will be determined partly by the length of the curriculum. Of course we cannot expect, in a simple, common school, to pursue theology, or any other branch, with the thoroughness with which it should be pursued at a university. It will also depend, partly, upon the circumstances of the individual scholar. A boy who intends to pass his whole life in some mechanical trade, or in a storehouse, should not be expected to study theology to such an extent as one who gives evidence of an ability and a desire to become a public teacher, whether in the schoolhouse or the church. But, with either scholar, the due proportion of directly religious instruction should be determined by this general principle, that sufficient should be given to lead the pupil to see at least the religious bearing of his other knowledge, be that other knowledge much or little,—that he may neither build too much upon an insecure foundation, nor fail to raise the most worthy structure which his basis and his capital will allow.

In like manner the questions in regard to the form of religion may be answered. The statutes of that State in which I passed the first years of my manhood, make it imperative on the teachers of the common schools to teach good manners and morals. This is teaching religion practically. In the earlier years of school life this is right;—it is the course of nature, and precisely analogous to the course which I would recommend in the teaching of other departments of learning. But as the child grows older, it should learn abstract forms of words as well as practical rules; and in colleges, should have a certain amount of direct studies in natural and revealed religion, moral science, and dogmatic theology,—regard of course being had to the general principles before stated, with reference to the amount.

The question may, however, be pressed upon me, concerning the form of religion to be taught; whether it should be distinctly Christian or not, and if Christian, whether it should be distinctly Protestant or not. If Protestant, shall it be Calvinistic, Arminian, or Pelagian? The usual answers to such questions seem to me founded upon fallacious arguments. The objections to sectarian teachings, and to intolerance of other forms of faith, are valid; but are very generally placed upon what I consider invalid grounds, or at least upon secondary grounds, while more fundamental considerations would more effectually settle the point.

It is frequently said that politics and religion should be excluded from our common schools, and other institutions of public instruction, because they are matters upon which men's opinions are divided; that politics taught in a school must necessarily offend the partisans of opposite views, and religion taught in the schools must necessarily wound the conscience of those whose doctrines differ from those of the text-books. Others have replied that there are common opinions in these matters, which it would be well to teach; opinions in which all the world are agreed, and which are therefore suitable to be the theme of public instruction.

That such considerations should be only of secondary weight in deciding the great questions under discussion, will be at once manifest when we apply them to the test at the other end of the hierarchy. There are many mathematical and mechanical points, long in dispute among the learned, and upon some of them there is not a perfect agreement even to this day. The foundation of all geometry is in our idea of space, and even that is a subject of irreconcilable differences of opinion. The followers of the immortal Kant (and even many of those who in most things else break away from his paths, follow him here), declare that space has no existence other than in the mind of the observer, and some of them further affirm that it is an idea never attained by those born blind. Space, according to these philosophers (and I think they comprise a majority of those who have shown a decided turn for metaphysical speculation), is only a way in which we view things; it is a law of thought, and the proof that it is so, lies in the fact that we necessarily conceive of things as occupying space. Since we cannot even mentally divest ourselves of the idea of space, it must be, say these men, a part of ourselves and non-existent out of ourselves.

On the contrary, many geometricians of the highest ability believe, as all ordinary men believe, in the reality of space external to the mind. To them the doctrine of "the laws of thought," the doctrine that space and time are forms put upon things by the mind, appears the very quixotism of philosophy. It amounts to saying that we know that space does not exist because we cannot help believing that it does exist.

But, while the fundamental conceptions of geometry, while the very existence of its subject-matter, space, is thus in dispute, and the learned world so equally divided on the point, is geometry to be excluded from the course of public instruction, or shall any believer in space hesitate in his public teaching to proclaim his faith, and to utter his protest against the transcendental delusions and errors which have accompanied the growth of transcendental philosophy? Certainly no man would ask it.

Again, there are those who deny that space is the subject-matter of geometry. The French school of positive philosophy say that geometry is the science of measuring extended bodies. Our own countryman, H. C. Carey, in the introductory chapters of his splendid work on Social Science, denies to geometry the name of science. Science, he says, is the knowledge of external nature, and the mathematics is only a peculiar language to aid in investigating nature and recording results. With still grosser ideas, another American writer maintains that a line is an infinitesimal thread, and a point an atom, thus reducing geometry to the science of extended bodies considered as extended.

Does, therefore, any teacher think that we should not carefully guard the student of geometry from supposing that he is studying either material shapes or mere abstract rules of measuring material things?

The like conclusion, that the mere fact of the existence of differences of opinion concerning a science, does not unfit it to take its place in a course of public instruction, might be drawn from all the other sciences. We frequently find men, through a deficiency of mathematical clearness, opposing the Newtonian doctrine of gravity, and stating new theories of mechanics; — or putting out new ideas concerning optics. Even in the Reports of the Proceedings of the American Association for the Advancement of Science, you will find a paper explaining the zodiacal light, the whole paper being based on the astounding assumption that both ends of a straight line may be far below the horizon, and yet a large part of the line remain above the horizon.

I might go into chemistry and find still more striking instances of differences of opinion. I need not allude to bygones, such as the contest concerning the nature of chlorine, — but may appeal to the present state of the science. Who shall set bounds to the doctrines of allotropism, and assure us that the whole list of elemental substances is not after all but a series of allotropic forms of one and the same substance? Yet if this be so, who shall be able to define the science of chemistry? Nevertheless the science is pursued and taught and justly considered an essential element in a course of public instruction. It is even demanded as a practical science for the use of agriculturists, although the most vital points concerning the value of mineral and organic manures are still in dispute. We may therefore set it down as certain, that differences of opinion concerning the truth or falsehood of a doctrine do not constitute, in the judgment of wise men, any reason for omitting the discussion of those doctrines from the course of public instruction. Nor, on the other hand, is perfect unanimity of opinion upon a point, or perfect certainty of a doctrine, any reason why such points should be included in our general course of study. No mathematician doubts the truth, or the utility, of that little book on the division of superficies, published by John Dee and Frederic Commandine, and thought by Dee to be from the hand of the great Euclid, but no one has ever proposed to incorporate it, or any part of it, into a course of academical study.

It is, therefore, manifest that the questions of certainty or uncertainty, and difference or unity of opinion, are only secondary considerations in deciding whether a certain study should or should not enter into the course of instruction in this or that form.

The general principles which I have already enunciated concerning the relation of each part to the whole, and to the whole hierarchy of sciences, to the length of the curriculum, and to the capacities of the individuals, these general principles are sufficient to decide the minor as well as the greater questions. Those parts of geometry are to be introduced which bear most directly upon the progress of the student in higher mathematical studies, and to the acquirement of mechanical, chemical, botanical, or zoölogical knowledge. Those parts are to be excluded which are not thus connected. And inasmuch as no knowledge is wholly disconnected with other branches (the work to which I just alluded as resuscitated by Dee, is capable of some useful applications in surveying, etc.), we must omit those things which have fewest or least important connections, and retain those which are most directly in the highway of truth.

So in religion. It makes no essential difference whether there is, or is not, an agreement of opinion on a point; it does not necessarily follow that it is important if all are agreed, or that it is unimportant if men are disagreed upon it. The question rather is, Is this doctrine important in its connection with other matters? Does it throw light on the course of history? Does it have a connection with the physical sciences? Does it bear directly on the moral character of the pupil? Does it bear upon his religious character, his habits of piety?

We have tested, on such general principles, the question whether religion ought, or ought not, to enter into the course of public instruction, and have decided that it should. But shall we teach Theism or Atheism, Pantheism or Exotheism? By the last term, I designate that steadfast ignoring of religious questions to which an exclusive attachment to physical researches may lead one. But this and blank Atheism we have already condemned as unfit to be taught anywhere, or by anybody; Atheism, because it denies the central truth of all science, the truth which alone makes science possible, destroying thus the natural head of the whole hierarchy of sciences; Exotheism, because it steadily puts this central truth of all science out of view, and attempts to degrade theology from its natural position of the head of the sciences, and to place it in a subordinate position among "oldwives' fables."

It remains, then, to consider whether we should teach Pantheism or Monotheism. Now, to me, Pantheism is, in theology, very much like the doctrine that in geometry we have only logical forms of thought, and are not dealing with entities. To teach such geometry seriously and earnestly, is better than to deride the science altogether; but it does not develop the powers of imagination and conception; it does not link itself with all the higher branches of science so well as the higher doctrine that geometry is the science treating of the real subject-matter—space. So, a reverent and devout Pantheism may be better than Atheism, and even better than the Exotheism of positive science. For, as the language of a devout spirit, even when intellectually misled towards Pantheism, is theistic, the mind of the pupil may receive the higher truth, through the medium intended by the teacher to convey only the lower truth. But Monotheistic views alone give theology its true position in the scale of sciences. With Pantheistic views the highest science is lower than one of inferior grade. When on going upward through the sciences we have at last studied in the human mind the laws of thought and feeling and volition, we perceive that this self-conscious mind is the highest object of our thought yet found. But as we have seen, while studying the material universe, innumerable evidences of wisdom, of plan and of purpose, we must suppose an Infinite mind ruling the great mass of matter. But here comes the question, Does this great mind which adapts all organs to their functions, all materials to their uses, all forms to the fulfilment of an ideal plan, do so consciously or unconsciously? In other words, when we rise from the contemplation of our minds to the contemplation of the Infinite mind, do we fall from the consideration of a conscious being, to the consideration of an unconscious being? To me it seems that this question answers itself by its own absurdity. The modern philosophy which regards the universe as an unconscious struggle of non-being to become being, saved only by that struggle from relapsing into the pure zero of non-existence, saved only by the impossibility of succeeding in the struggle, from going over to the pure zero (as they term it) of being, seems to me to be itself the pure zero of irrationality, — which would be shocking to our sentiments of reverence, if it were only sufficiently intelligible to be comprehended. To us who believe in the first article of the creed, that there is one God, the Father Almighty, maker of heaven and earth, that article is by far the most important of all truths; and it is on this account that we insist it should make a fundamental point in the instruction of youth, and cannot concede that on any grounds it should be omitted.

The second article of the creed is also one which must be considered, by those who believe in it, an article of fundamental importance. No man, indeed, can deny that faith in the revelation made through our Lord Jesus Christ, must assume, in the mind of one who holds it, a central position — controlling and modifying all his course of thought. Our entire views of theology and morality are dependent on the views we take of Christ, and we cannot, therefore, put Christianity among the unimportant parts of religious instruction. That some disbelieve in it, and that there is warmth of feeling connected with the discussion of its truth, cannot justify us in omitting the subject, any more than the differences of opinion upon questions of chemistry, physiology, and geology, would justify a teacher of those sciences in omitting all reference to allotropism, to therapeutic agencies, or to glacial and diluvial action. The evidences of Christianity occupy a central position in theology, which is a fundamental science; and those to whom these evidences are sufficient are justified on every conceivable ground in assuming always in their public instruction the authority of the New Testament; and whenever their school is of such a nature as to permit it, in showing with some minuteness the various branches of evidence that tend to establish the fact that Jesus was proved to be the Son of God with power by his resurrection from the dead, and by wondrous works that no man could have done except God were with him. I am well aware that there are persons at the present day who claim to have outgrown the necessity of attending to this evidence; some by having grown so spiritual that the religious truths proclaimed by our Lord commend themselves directly to their minds and hearts as true, as needing no external proofs of having been uttered by authority; others, by having grown too wise to be convinced by such proofs, who have set up for themselves new canons of criticism that render the falsehood of the gospels demonstrable, and who therefore justify themselves in passing by all the evidences of their truth. I am well aware of the existence of these persons to whom and for whom the evidences of Christianity are nothing, and who would claim that in consideration of their existence, we should omit all distinctively Christian instruction from our public course of education. But I do not see how their requirements should be granted, any more than I see why the existence of persons incapable of receiving the Newtonian laws of philosophy should cause us to omit the recognition of those laws from our text-books on physics. In order to omit Christianity and the evidences of its truth from our course of studies, we must show, not that there is not a perfect unanimity of opinion upon the matter, but that it is a question which does not connect itself vitally with our views of history, — which does not throw light upon any physical sciences, — which does not bear directly upon the moral character of the pupil, — which does not affect his religious character, his habitual tone of thought on religious things. Now no sane man, however strong he may feel himself in his rejection of Christ, can deny that the question of the reality of the revelation through Jesus does connect itself, vitally, with all our views of history. According to the believer in revelation, all previous events prepared the way for the coming of Christ, all succeeding events have been modified by it, and Calvary is the central point in the great historic picture of this world. Even the unbeliever in Christ must acknowledge that never man spake like that man; that never did the word of prophet or sage produce so sudden, so extensive, and so lasting an effect upon civilized and enlightened nations as that produced by the preaching of the gospel. What think ye of Christ, is therefore a fundamental question in the survey of human history.

Neither can any sane man deny that our reception or rejection of Christ affects our views of physical science. If we reject Him, then we are naturally led to reject the views which he gives us of the freedom, the sovereignty, and the forgiving love of God; if we accept Him, we of course accept these views, and are ready to receive the doctrines of geology which declare that God has frequently acted upon our planet in circumscribed limits and at definite times, fulfilling through the long course of geological changes one plan, which He had in view from the beginning, the preparation of the earth for the abode of his children, — those doctrines of physics which find in all material things the expressions of wisdom and of personal kindness, — those doctrines of history which recognize a ruling Providence, and devoutly acknowledge that

> "There 's a divinity that shapes our ends,
> Rough hew them as we will."

No sane man can deny that the reception or rejection of Christ will naturally have a tendency to affect the moral character of the pupil. To reject him and his doctrines, — to claim that he was inspired in no other sense and in no other degree than we may each of us be inspired, if we will pay the price, — what can be the effect upon us if not to weaken in us the sentiment of reverence, and to strengthen out of due proportion the consciousness of our own dignity and worth? But to admit the authority of Jesus, — to acknowledge and open our hearts to the love of Him who though he was rich yet for our sakes became poor, who though clothed with divine powers did not ask divine honors, but submitted to poverty, to suffering, and to death, in patient attestation of his mission, still offering forgiveness and help from God to those who were seeking his life; to admit the authority of such a master,— what can its natural tendency be, if not to soften the fiercer passions of the believer, and to bring him, at least partially, into a likeness of this divine example?

Nor can any sane man deny that the acceptance or rejection of the claims of Jesus to direct authority from God, must in general have a marked effect upon the religious character of the pupil. Few men have that strength and depth of religious character, which can make them, after rejecting the claims of Jesus to direct authority, feel that in their own souls they have a direct vision of religious truth,—a direct internal vision of the presence of an infinite Father. With by far the larger part of the human race, experience has shown that if they do not see God revealed in the face of Jesus Christ, they do not see him clearly at all; their rejection of Jesus' authority is usually, and I think naturally, followed by their neglect of Jesus' precept to pray, by their disbelief in his doctrine of a special Providence, and finally, by a rejection of his doctrine of the Fatherhood of God. When a man rejects the evidences of Christianity, he usually, and I think naturally, slides towards Pantheistic views of the divine nature.

It must therefore, I hold, be conceded on all sides, that the Christian religion is of such importance, in its connection with physical, historical, metaphysical, moral, and religious truth, as to demand a place in every scheme of public instruction, in spite of the acknowledged fact that there are those who reject its claims to be a revealed religion. But if we bring it into our public instruction, how shall we bring it in, as believers or as unbelievers? Surely those who disagree with us in our convictions would not ask us to teach what we think falsehood. If it is, as I have endeavored to show, necessary for us to speak on religious themes, and to discuss the claims of Christ as the Messiah, the King of the new kingdom of God, we must of course speak as we believe. It may be right for us to acknowledge to our pupils the existence of other opinions; it may even be right for us to show to them the reasons adduced by unbelievers for rejecting the gospels. But it is certainly more imperative upon us, according to all the principles which regulate the sphere of education, to show our pupils the reasons for thinking the arguments of unbelievers delusive sophistry, our reasons for thinking that the evidence of the resurrection of Jesus Christ from the dead is stronger than the evidence for any other historical fact whatever. We are bound, by every principle which can actuate or guide us in the sphere of education, to express to our pupils our view of the labors of the great schools of historical, philological, and metaphysical critics; our conviction that, upon either and each of these three grounds, the rationalistic party, rejecting the supernatural character of the gospel, are inexpressibly weak and sophistical; the supernatural party, admitting the claims of Jesus, are invincibly strong, not in themselves, but in the overwhelming strength of their arguments, appealing not to hair-splitting distinctions and refined quibbling, but to the common sense of honest hearts. Taking the view which we do of the connection of the fundamental Christian doctrine, that Jesus is the Christ, with all other truth, we must introduce it into public instruction, and, being believers, must of course introduce it as believers.

What then, it may be asked, is to hinder this course of reasoning from justifying the introduction of sectarian strife into our schools and colleges? Do not each sect of Christians claim that their peculiarities are fundamental doctrines, and must be considered a part of Christianity?

I answer, No! There is no sect of Christians who will not confess that in the hearty and humble recognition of the Apostle's Creed lies all that is fundamental in Christianity. The greatest diversities perhaps existing in the Christian church, are those between Augustine's views and those of Pelagius on predestination and freewill; and those between Papists, Congregationalists, and the New Jerusalem Church, on the source of the light by which we are to read the Scriptures. These diversities are so great and so nearly fundamental, that they doubtless affect in some degree our views of truth in other matters. In a Sunday school they may be taught, and in a theological school they must be thoroughly discussed; there are, indeed, those who feel that these points are sufficiently important in their bearing upon the whole field of culture, to demand their introduction into colleges. Hence we have, in various parts of the country, colleges under the special patronage of particular sects of the Christian church. If any man feel that the importance of these views is great enough to demand their introduction into the college course, he is of course right in sustaining such colleges. But the highest authorities can be quoted from those holding each of the five different opinions which I have named, to the effect that their own opinions are not absolutely essential to the Gospel, but that their opponents may hold the essential body of Christian truth in spite of their error; and hence those opinions cannot be of sufficient importance to claim their introduction into the common schools.

The points on which the various sects differ are, in general, very much less important than the five points of predestination, freewill, the right of private judgment, the authority of the church to interpret Scripture, and the claims of Emanuel Swedenborg, and if these five are not of sufficient importance to demand their introduction into the common school, of course no other point of sectarian division is worthy of that honor. We must remember that the human mind is not capable of attending to an unlimited number of things at once. In the growing mind we must, it is true, introduce a due proportion of each of the great divisions of science; but to do justice to all we must not show a favoritism toward any. In the balancing of a just course of study, great prominence must be given to the essential doctrines of Christianity, those which are acknowledged by all to be the most essential, the most characteristic; and if the points about which the sects are divided are brought in, then one of two evils follows; these minor points either distract the mind from other and more essential parts of religion, or distract it from other studies equally important in a liberal or public education.

The conclusion at which I arrive is therefore this, That into the public course of instruction in our Christian land it is our privilege and our duty to introduce the Christian religion in a positive and earnest form, adapted to the ages of the pupils and to the length of the course of studies on which they have entered, but that the dogmas concerning which Christians differ should not be introduced, but be reserved for theological schools,—and that these conclusions flow not only nor chiefly from considerations concerning the certainty or doubtfulness of such dogmas, but from considerations of their relative

importance and from general principles concerning the choice of studies, which govern wise instructors in all lower branches.

MEMBERS OF THE GRADUATING CLASS, —

It is hard for me to believe that the deep interest with which many of you followed for two months the exposition of the evidences of Christianity, was not shared in some degree by you all. I cannot but believe that in the essays which you gave me at the close of that study you expressed the real convictions of your hearts, and that you join me in heartily believing that the apostles followed no cunningly devised fables, but were the eye-witnesses of the majesty of Christ, and bore testimony to that which they had themselves seen and handled. Let me then, as the application of this address to your case, and as the parting word of my instruction to you in Antioch Hall, beseech you to become, whatever your choice of a profession, or occupation in life, teachers of the religion of Jesus. An educated man is, voluntarily or involuntarily, whatever his walk in life, a teacher by word and by example. Be it your care, graduates from this Hall, consecrated by the prayers of saints, consecrated by the life and death of that hero, whose place I imperfectly attempt to fill, be it your care that your teaching shall lead those with whom you have intercourse, to honor and embrace that gospel which they see sanctifying your daily

deeds and words. So alone shall you fulfil the highest office to which you have been called, and so alone receive, when graduating from the school of life, honors from the Great Teacher of all.

www.ingramcontent.com/pod-product-compliance
Lightning Source LLC
LaVergne TN
LVHW011133110826
845150LV00008B/2315
* 9 7 8 1 4 1 8 1 9 3 9 8 0 *